# fish &
# seafood

simple and delicious easy-to-make recipes

June Hammond

p

This is a Parragon Publishing Book

First Published in 2002

Parragon Publishing
Queen Street House
4 Queen Street
Bath, BA1 1HE, UK

Copyright © Parragon 2002

ISBN: 0-75258-868-0

Printed in China

Produced by the Bridgewater Book Company Ltd.

**Photographer** Calvey Taylor-Haw

**Home Economist** Ricky Taylor

## NOTES FOR THE READER

- This book uses both imperial and metric measurements. Follow the same units of measurement throughout; do not mix imperial and metric.

- All spoon measurements are level: teaspoons are assumed to be 5 ml, and tablespoons are assumed to be 15 ml.

- Unless otherwise stated, milk is assumed to be whole milk, eggs and individual vegetables such as potatoes are medium, and pepper is freshly ground black pepper.

- Recipes using raw or very lightly cooked eggs should be avoided by infants, the elderly, pregnant women, convalescents, and anyone suffering from an illness.

- The times given are an approximate guide only. Preparation times differ according to the techniques used by different people and the cooking times may also vary from those given. Optional ingredients, variations, or serving suggestions have not been included in the calculations.

# contents

# introduction

Fish and shellfish are superbly healthy foods. Always buy and use only the freshest fish and shellfish, and you will find that their value in terms of health, quality, and flavor is hard to beat. They are low in calories, yet rich in nutrients such as B vitamins and proteins. Oily fish in particular, such as salmon and anchovies, are a good source of omega-3 oils, which the body cannot produce for itself. These oils have anti-inflammatory properties and are believed to be very beneficial for maintaining a healthy heart.

Fish and shellfish are excellent sources of other nutrients too, such as iodine, which is essential for a healthy thyroid gland and efficient metabolism; co-enzyme Q10, which strengthens muscle and protects against heart disease and diabetes; zinc, which is essential in the synthesis of DNA and helps repair tissue; and magnesium, which plays an important role in the formation of bone, and in energy production and insulin regulation.

Many types of fish and shellfish, such as cod and tuna, shrimp and mussels, are low in fat, and can be invaluable as part of a weight control regime. But most of all, we shouldn't forget that fish is delicious and wonderfully versatile. So whatever the occasion, there will be something here to satisfy every palate.

| guide to recipe key | | |
|---|---|---|
| | very easy | Recipes are graded as follows: 1 pea = easy; 2 peas = very easy; 3 peas = extremely easy. |
| | serves 4 | Recipes generally serve four people. Simply halve the ingredients to serve two, taking care not to mix imperial and metric measurements. |
| | 10 minutes | Preparation time. Where marinating, chilling, or cooling are involved, these times have been added on separately: eg, 15 minutes + 30 minutes to marinate. |
| | 10 minutes | Cooking time. Cooking times don't include the cooking of side dishes or accompaniments served with the main dishes. |

cod & sweet potato soup
page 10

shrimp cocktail
page 36

crab & citrus salsa
page 56

salmon with brandy sauce
page 72

# soups & stews

Fish soups make a delicious start to any meal, or a light meal in themselves when served with some fresh crusty bread and salad greens. And when appetites are large, what could be more satisfying than a simmering fish stew full of tantalizing flavors and mouthwatering ingredients? This chapter presents a collection of recipes with international flavors from countries such as France, Spain, and Thailand, and all are quick and easy to make.

# haddock soup à la provençal

| | | ingredients | |
|---|---|---|---|
| | very easy | 1 tbsp extra-virgin olive oil | generous ¼ cup red wine |
| | | 2 red onions, chopped | 4 cups vegetable bouillon |
| | serves 4 | 2 garlic cloves, finely chopped | 1 bay leaf |
| | | 1 carrot, chopped | 12 oz/350 g haddock fillets, skinned |
| | | 1 red bell pepper, seeded and chopped | salt and pepper |
| | 15 minutes | 6 tomatoes | fresh basil, chopped, to garnish |
| | | 1 tbsp tomato paste | |
| | | 1 tsp turmeric | slices of French bread, to serve |
| | 1 hour 10 minutes | | |

Heat the oil in a large pan over medium heat. Add the onions and cook, stirring from time to time, for about 4 minutes. Add the garlic, carrot, bell pepper, tomatoes, tomato paste, and turmeric and cook, stirring occasionally, for another 4 minutes. Stir in the wine, then the bouillon. Add the bay leaf and bring to a boil. Lower the heat and simmer for 25 minutes, stirring occasionally.

Rinse the haddock fillets under cold running water, then add them to the soup. Season with salt and pepper and cook for another 25 minutes until the fish is cooked through.

Remove the pan from the heat, let the soup cool a little, then discard the bay leaf. Transfer the soup to a food processor and process until smooth (you may need to do this in batches). Return the soup to the pan and bring gently to a boil again. Lower the heat and simmer for 5 minutes, then pour the soup into serving bowls, garnish with fresh basil, and serve with French bread.

# cod & sweet potato soup

| | |
|---|---|
| very easy | |
| serves 4 | |
| 15 minutes + 30 minutes to marinate | |
| 40 minutes | |

### ingredients

4 tbsp lemon juice
1 red chile, seeded and finely sliced
pinch of nutmeg
9 oz/250 g cod fillets, skinned
1 tbsp vegetable oil
1 onion, chopped
4 scallions, trimmed and chopped
2 garlic cloves, chopped
1 lb/450 g sweet potatoes, diced

4 cups vegetable bouillon
salt and pepper
1 carrot, sliced
5½ oz/150 g white cabbage, shredded
2 celery stalks, trimmed and sliced

fresh crusty bread, to serve

Put the lemon juice, chile, and nutmeg into a shallow, nonmetallic (glass or ceramic) dish and mix to make a marinade. Rinse the cod, cut it into chunks, and add to the bowl. Turn in the marinade until coated. Cover with plastic wrap and let marinate for 30 minutes.

Heat the oil in a large pan over medium heat. Add the onion and scallions and cook, stirring, for 4 minutes. Add the garlic and cook for 2 minutes.

Add the diced sweet potatoes, pour in the bouillon, and season. Bring to a boil, lower the heat, cover, and simmer for 10 minutes. Add the carrot, cabbage, and celery, and simmer for 8–10 minutes. Remove from the heat and allow to cool a little.

Process the soup in a food processor until smooth (you may need to do this in batches), then return to the pan. Add the fish chunks and marinade and bring gently to a boil. Lower the heat and simmer for 10 minutes. Ladle the soup into bowls and serve with crusty bread.

# bouillabaisse

| | | ingredients | |
|---|---|---|---|
| easy | | 9 oz/250 g cod or haddock fillets | 1 bay leaf |
| | | 9 oz/250 g sea bass fillets | pinch of saffron threads |
| serves 4 | | 6 tbsp olive oil | 5$\frac{1}{2}$ oz/150 g potatoes |
| | | 4 garlic cloves, chopped | 3$\frac{1}{2}$ oz/100 g live mussels, soaked and |
| | | 2 onions, sliced | cleaned (see page 20) |
| | | 1 small red chile, seeded and chopped | 3$\frac{1}{2}$ oz/100 g scallops |
| 20 minutes | | 2 celery stalks, trimmed and sliced | 10$\frac{1}{2}$ oz/300 g shrimp, peeled and |
| | | 1 green bell pepper, seeded and sliced | deveined |
| | | 4 tomatoes, sliced | fresh parsley, chopped, to garnish |
| 1 hour 10 minutes | | 4 cups fish bouillon | |
| | | scant $\frac{1}{2}$ cup dry white wine | slices of French bread, to serve |

Rinse the fish fillets, cut into chunks, and put them in a shallow dish. Mix 3 tablespoons of oil with 1 chopped garlic clove and pour over the fish. Cover with plastic wrap and refrigerate. Heat 1 tablespoon of oil in a pan. Add 1 onion and the chile, celery, and bell pepper. Cook over medium heat for 4 minutes. Add the tomatoes, bouillon, wine, bay leaf, and saffron. Bring to a boil, cover, and simmer for 30 minutes. Strain and reserve the liquid. Heat the remaining oil in a pan. Add the remaining garlic and onion and cook for 4 minutes. Slice and add the potatoes and strained bouillon. Bring to a boil, lower the heat to medium, cover, and cook for 15 minutes.

Put the mussels in a pan with a little water, bring to a boil, and cook over high heat for 4 minutes. Discard any that remain closed. Add the fish chunks to the potato pan. Cook for 2 minutes. Add the mussels, scallops, and shrimp. Cook for 4 minutes. Transfer to serving bowls, garnish with parsley, and serve with slices of French bread.

# thai shrimp & scallop soup

| | | ingredients | |
|---|---|---|---|
| very easy | | 4 cups fish bouillon | 8 oz/225 g shrimp, peeled and |
| | | juice of $\frac{1}{2}$ lime | deveined |
| serves 4 | | 2 tbsp rice wine or sherry | 8 oz/225 g scallops |
| | | 1 leek, trimmed and chopped | 1$\frac{1}{2}$ tbsp chopped fresh flatleaf parsley |
| | | 2 shallots, finely chopped | salt and pepper |
| 5 minutes | | 1 tbsp grated fresh gingerroot | fresh flatleaf parsley, chopped, |
| | | 1 red chile, seeded and finely chopped | to garnish |
| 15 minutes | | | |

Put the bouillon, lime juice, rice wine or sherry, leek, shallots, ginger, and chile into a large pan. Bring to a boil, then lower the heat, cover, and simmer for 10 minutes.

Add the shrimp, scallops, and parsley, season with salt and pepper, and cook for about 1–2 minutes.

Remove the pan from the heat, ladle the soup into serving bowls, garnish with chopped fresh parsley, and serve.

# chorizo & scallop soup

| | | ingredients | |
|---|---|---|---|
| very easy | | 4½ oz/125 g lean chorizo, skinned and chopped | ½ tsp dried oregano |
| | | 1 lb/450 g yellow field peas | salt and pepper |
| serves 4 | | 1 tbsp vegetable oil | 8 oz/225 g scallops |
| | | 2 shallots, chopped | |
| | | 2 carrots, chopped | fresh flatleaf parsley, chopped, to garnish |
| 10 minutes | | 2 leeks, trimmed and chopped | |
| | | 2 garlic cloves, chopped | slices of fresh whole-wheat bread, to serve |
| 1¼–1½ hours | | 6¼ cups vegetable bouillon | |

Put the chorizo in a clean, dry skillet and cook over medium heat for about 5–8 minutes. Lift out with a perforated spoon and drain on paper towels. Put the peas in a strainer and rinse under cold running water. Let drain.

Heat the oil in a large pan over medium heat. Add the shallots and cook for about 4 minutes, until slightly softened. Add the carrots, leeks, and garlic, and cook for another 3 minutes.

Add the drained peas to the pan, then the bouillon and oregano. Bring to a boil, then add the chorizo and season with salt and pepper. Lower the heat, cover, and simmer for 1–1¼ hours. Just before the end of the cooking time, add the scallops and cook for about 2 minutes.

Remove the pan from the heat. Ladle the soup into serving bowls, garnish with chopped fresh parsley, and serve with slices of fresh whole-wheat bread.

# spicy crab & vegetable soup

| | | **ingredients** | |
|---|---|---|---|
| | very easy | 1 lb 2 oz/500 g tomatoes | 7 oz/200 g canned or freshly cooked |
| | | 4 cups fish or vegetable bouillon | crab meat |
| | | 4 tsp red wine | 5½ oz/150 g canned corn kernels |
| | serves 4 | 5½ oz/150 g red cabbage, shredded | 4 tbsp chopped fresh flatleaf parsley |
| | | 2 red onions, sliced | salt and pepper |
| | | 2 carrots, cut into short, thin sticks | |
| | 15 minutes | 3 garlic cloves, chopped | fresh flatleaf parsley, chopped, |
| | | 1 small red chile, seeded and finely | to garnish |
| | | chopped | fresh crusty baguettes, to serve |
| | 35 minutes | 1 bay leaf | |

Put the tomatoes into a heatproof bowl, cover with boiling water, and let stand for 1 minute. Drain, plunge into cold water, then remove the skins—they should come off easily.

Chop the tomatoes, then put them into a large pan. Pour over the bouillon, then add the wine, cabbage, onions, carrots, garlic, chile, and bay leaf. Bring to a boil, then lower the heat and simmer for about 15 minutes.

Add the crab meat, corn, and parsley to the pan, and season with salt and plenty of pepper. Cook gently over low heat for another 15 minutes.

Remove the pan from the heat and discard the bay leaf. Ladle the soup into serving bowls, garnish with chopped fresh parsley, and serve with fresh crusty baguettes.

# fruits de mer stew

| | | ingredients | |
|---|---|---|---|
| easy | | 3 tbsp olive oil | 1½ cups fish bouillon |
| | | 2 garlic cloves, chopped | 4 tbsp red wine |
| | | 3 scallions, trimmed and chopped | salt and pepper |
| serves 4 | | 1 red bell pepper, seeded and chopped | 7 oz/200 g canned crab meat |
| | | 15 oz/425 g canned chopped tomatoes | 7 oz/200 g shrimp, peeled and deveined |
| | | 1 tbsp tomato paste | 9 oz/250 g cooked lobster meat |
| 15 minutes | | 1 bay leaf | |
| | | ½ tsp dried mixed herbs | GARNISH |
| | | 7 oz/200 g live mussels | fresh flatleaf parsley, chopped |
| | | 5½ oz/150 g cod fillet, skinned | slices of lemon |
| 30 minutes | | 5½ oz/150 g swordfish steak, skinned | slices of French bread, to serve |

Heat the oil in a pan over low heat. Add the garlic, scallions, and bell pepper and cook, stirring, for 4 minutes. Add the tomatoes, tomato paste, bay leaf, and mixed herbs. Cook for 10 minutes.

Meanwhile, soak the mussels in lightly salted water for 10 minutes. Scrub under cold running water and pull off any beards. Discard any with broken shells. Tap the remaining mussels and discard any that refuse to close. Put them in a large pan with a little water, bring to a boil, and cook over high heat for 4 minutes. Remove from the heat and discard any mussels that remain closed.

Cut the cod and swordfish into chunks and add to the tomato pan. Add the bouillon and wine. Season and bring to a boil. Add the mussels and crab, lower the heat, cover, and cook for 5 minutes. Add the shrimp and cook for 3 minutes. Cut the lobster into chunks, add to the pan, and cook for 2 minutes. Transfer to bowls, garnish with parsley and lemon slices, and serve with slices of French bread.

# spanish swordfish stew

| | | ingredients | |
|---|---|---|---|
| very easy | | 4 tbsp olive oil | 1 orange bell pepper, seeded and |
| | | 3 shallots, chopped | chopped |
| serves 4 | | 2 garlic cloves, chopped | 20 black olives, pitted and halved |
| | | 8 oz/225 g canned chopped tomatoes | 2 lb 4 oz/1 kg swordfish steak, skinned |
| | | 1 tbsp tomato paste | and cut into bite-size pieces |
| | | 1 lb 7 oz/650 g potatoes, sliced | salt and pepper |
| 10 minutes | | 1 cup vegetable bouillon | |
| | | 2 tbsp lemon juice | GARNISH |
| | | 1 red bell pepper, seeded and chopped | sprigs of fresh flatleaf parsley |
| | | | slices of lemon |
| 55 minutes | | | |
| | | | fresh crusty bread, to serve |

Heat the oil in a pan over low heat. Add the shallots and cook, stirring occasionally, for about 4 minutes, until slightly softened. Add the garlic, tomatoes, and tomato paste, cover, and cook gently for 20 minutes.

Put the potatoes into a flameproof casserole with the bouillon and lemon juice. Bring to a boil, then lower the heat and add the bell peppers. Cover and cook for 15 minutes.

Add the olives, swordfish, and the tomato mixture to the potatoes. Season with salt and pepper. Stir the stew, cover, and simmer for 7–10 minutes, or until the swordfish is cooked to your taste.

Remove from the heat and garnish with sprigs of fresh parsley and lemon slices. Serve with fresh crusty bread.

# salads

Whoever said that salads are dull? This chapter offers some exciting recipes for you to try. For example, the Anchovy & Olive Salad shows just how well olives and fish go together, and the Warm Tuna & Kidney Bean Salad demonstrates how salads can be every bit as warming as a hot meal. Some salads in this chapter are light dishes that would make excellent appetizers or accompaniments to entrées. Others have extra ingredients added, such as tenderly cooked pasta, to make them into more substantial meals.

# tuna & herbed fusilli salad

| | | ingredients | |
|---|---|---|---|
| | extremely easy | 7 oz/200 g dried fusilli | DRESSING |
| | | 1 red bell pepper, seeded and cut | 6 tbsp basil-flavored oil or extra-virgin |
| | | into fourths | olive oil |
| | serves 4 | 5½ oz/150 g fresh asparagus spears | 3 tbsp white wine vinegar |
| | | 1 red onion, sliced | 1 tbsp lime juice |
| | | 4 tomatoes, sliced | 1 tsp mustard |
| | 15 minutes | 7 oz/200 g canned tuna in brine, | 1 tsp honey |
| | | drained | 4 tbsp chopped fresh basil |
| | | | |
| | 15 minutes | | sprigs of fresh basil, to garnish |

Boil a large pan of lightly salted water. Cook the fusilli for
10 minutes, or according to the instructions on the package. The
pasta should be tender but firm to the bite. While it is cooking,
put the bell pepper fourths under a broiler and cook until the skins
begin to blacken. Transfer to a plastic bag, seal, and set aside.

Bring another pan of water to a boil and cook the asparagus for
4 minutes. Drain and plunge into cold water, then drain again.
Remove the pasta from the heat, drain, and set aside to cool. Take
the bell pepper fourths from the bag and remove the blackened
skins. Slice the bell peppers into strips.

To make the dressing, put all the ingredients into a large bowl and
stir together well. Add the pasta, bell pepper strips, asparagus,
onion, tomatoes, and tuna. Toss together gently, then divide
between serving bowls. Garnish with sprigs of basil and serve.

# smoked salmon,
## asparagus & avocado salad

| | | ingredients | |
|---|---|---|---|
| | very easy | 7 oz/200 g fresh asparagus spears | 4 tbsp extra-virgin olive oil |
| | | 1 large ripe avocado | 2 tbsp white wine vinegar |
| | serves 4 | 1 tbsp lemon juice | 1 tbsp lemon juice |
| | | large handful fresh arugula leaves | pinch of sugar |
| | | 8 oz/225 g smoked salmon slices | 1 tsp mustard |
| | 15 minutes | 1 red onion, finely sliced | GARNISH |
| | | 1 tbsp chopped fresh flatleaf parsley | sprigs of fresh flatleaf parsley |
| | | 1 tbsp chopped fresh chives | wedges of lemon |
| | 5 minutes | DRESSING | fresh whole-wheat bread, to serve |
| | | 1 garlic clove, chopped | |

Bring a large pan of salted water to a boil. Add the asparagus and cook for 4 minutes, then drain. Refresh under cold running water and drain again. Set aside to cool.

To make the dressing, combine all the ingredients in a small bowl and stir together well. Cut the avocado in half lengthwise, then remove and discard the pit and skin. Cut the flesh into bite-size pieces and brush with lemon juice to prevent discoloration.

To assemble the salad, arrange the arugula on individual serving plates and top with the asparagus and avocado. Cut the smoked salmon into strips and scatter over the top of the salad, then scatter over the onion and herbs. Drizzle over the dressing, then garnish with fresh parsley sprigs and lemon wedges. Serve with fresh whole-wheat bread.

# warm tuna & kidney bean salad

| | | **ingredients** | |
|---|---|---|---|
| extremely easy | | 4 fresh tuna steaks, about 6 oz/175 g each | DRESSING |
| | | 1 tbsp olive oil | 5 tbsp extra-virgin olive oil |
| serves 4 | | 7 oz/200 g canned kidney beans | 3 tbsp balsamic vinegar |
| | | 3½ oz/100 g canned corn kernels | 1 tbsp lime juice |
| | | 2 scallions, trimmed and thinly sliced | 1 garlic clove, chopped |
| 10 minutes | | | 1 tbsp chopped fresh cilantro |
| | | | salt and pepper |
| 5–10 minutes | | | GARNISH |
| | | | sprigs of fresh cilantro |
| | | | wedges of lime |

Preheat a heavy, ridged grill pan. While the pan is heating, brush the tuna steaks with olive oil, then season with salt and pepper. Cook the steaks for 2 minutes, then turn them over and cook on the other side for another 2 minutes, or according to your taste, but do not overcook. Remove from the heat and let cool slightly.

While the tuna is cooling, heat the kidney beans and corn according to the instructions on the cans, then drain.

To make the dressing, put all the ingredients into a small bowl and stir together well.

Put the kidney beans, corn, and scallions into a large bowl, pour over half of the dressing and mix together well. Divide the bean and corn salad between individual serving plates, then place a tuna steak on each one. Drizzle over the remaining dressing, garnish with sprigs of fresh cilantro and wedges of lime, and serve.

# anchovy & olive salad

| | | **ingredients** | |
|---|---|---|---|
| | extremely easy | large handful mixed lettuce leaves | DRESSING |
| | | 12 cherry tomatoes, halved | 4 tbsp extra-virgin olive oil |
| | serves 4 | 20 black olives, pitted and halved | 1 tbsp white wine vinegar |
| | | 6 canned anchovy fillets, drained and sliced | 1 tbsp lemon juice |
| | | 1 tbsp chopped fresh oregano | 1 tbsp chopped fresh flatleaf parsley |
| | 10 minutes | | salt and pepper |
| | | | wedges of lemon, to garnish |
| | — | | |

To make the dressing, put all the ingredients into a small bowl, season with salt and pepper, and stir together well.

To assemble the salad, arrange the lettuce leaves in a serving dish. Scatter the cherry tomatoes on top, followed by the olives, anchovies, and oregano. Drizzle over the dressing. Serve on individual plates garnished with lemon wedges.

# seafood & spinach salad

| | |
|---|---|
| very easy | |
| serves 4 | |
| 25 minutes + 45 minutes to chill | |
| 10 minutes | |

## ingredients

1 lb 2 oz/500 g live mussels, soaked and cleaned (see page 20)
3 1/2 oz/100 g shrimp, peeled and deveined
12 oz/350 g scallops
1 lb 2 oz/500 g baby spinach leaves
3 scallions, trimmed and sliced

DRESSING
4 tbsp extra-virgin olive oil
2 tbsp white wine vinegar

1 tbsp lemon juice
1 tsp finely grated lemon zest
1 garlic clove, chopped
1 tbsp grated fresh gingerroot
1 small red chile, seeded and sliced
1 tbsp chopped fresh cilantro
salt and pepper

GARNISH
sprigs of fresh cilantro
wedges of lemon

Put the mussels into a large pan with a little water, bring to a boil, and cook over high heat for 4 minutes. Drain and reserve the liquid. Discard any mussels that remain closed. Return the reserved liquid to the pan and bring to a boil. Add the shrimp and scallops and cook for 3 minutes. Drain. Remove the mussels from their shells. Rinse the mussels, shrimp, and scallops in cold water, drain, and put them in a large bowl. Cool, cover with plastic wrap, and chill for 45 minutes. Meanwhile, rinse the baby spinach leaves and transfer them to a pan with 4 tablespoons of water. Cook over high heat for 1 minute, transfer to a strainer, refresh under cold running water, and drain.

To make the dressing, put all the ingredients into a small bowl and mix. Arrange the spinach on serving dishes, then scatter over half of the scallions. Top with the mussels, shrimp and scallops, then scatter over the remaining scallions. Drizzle over the dressing, garnish with fresh cilantro sprigs and wedges of lemon, and serve.

# shrimp cocktail

| | | **ingredients** |
|---|---|---|

| | | |
|---|---|---|
| very easy | 1 avocado<br>1 tbsp lemon juice<br>1 lb 2 oz/500 g cooked shrimp, peeled | 1 $\frac{1}{4}$ cups sunflower oil<br>scant $\frac{1}{2}$ cup tomato catsup |
| serves 4 | DRESSING<br>1 egg<br>2 tsp sherry vinegar<br>$\frac{1}{2}$ tsp mustard<br>dash of Worcestershire sauce<br>pinch of salt | GARNISH<br>pinch of paprika<br>thin strips of lemon zest<br>4 whole cooked shrimp, optional<br>fresh salad greens, to serve |
| 10 minutes | | |
| — | | |

To make the dressing, break the egg into a food processor. Add the vinegar, mustard, Worcestershire sauce, and salt, and process for 15 seconds. While the motor is running, slowly pour the sunflower oil through the feeder tube, until thoroughly incorporated. Transfer the dressing to a large bowl, then stir in the tomato catsup. Cover with plastic wrap and chill in the refrigerator until required.

Cut the avocado in half lengthwise, then remove and discard the pit and skin. Cut the flesh into slices, then brush the slices with lemon juice to prevent discoloration.

To assemble the salad, take the dressing from the refrigerator, add the avocado and shrimp, and stir gently until coated.

Divide the salad greens between large individual serving glasses or bowls. Fill each one with shrimp, then garnish with paprika and lemon zest strips. If using whole shrimp, hang a whole cooked shrimp on the rim of each glass or bowl. Serve immediately.

# light meals

Fish and shellfish make wonderful light meals. This chapter presents recipes with a wide range of international flavors from places as far apart as South America, Europe, and Asia. The dishes are all easy to prepare and quick to cook, and are full of nutritious ingredients. Some are deliciously light yet satisfying, such as Monkfish & Asparagus Stir-Fry, while others are irresistibly rich, such as Mediterranean Mussels in Cream. Many of these dishes would make superb lunches or light suppers.

# monkfish & asparagus stir-fry

| | | |
|---|---|---|
| very easy | | |
| serves 4 | | |
| 15 minutes | | |
| 15 minutes | | |

### ingredients

1 lb 2 oz/500 g monkfish
4 tbsp vegetable oil
2 zucchini, trimmed, halved, and sliced
1 red bell pepper, seeded and sliced
2 garlic cloves, finely chopped
5 1/2 oz/150 g fresh asparagus spears
3 1/2 oz/100 g snow peas

6 tbsp plain flour
4 tbsp lemon sauce (available ready-
made from supermarkets and Asian
grocery stores)
1 tbsp freshly grated lemongrass
1 tbsp grated fresh gingerroot
salt and pepper

Remove any membrane from the monkfish, then cut the flesh into thin slices. Cover the fish with plastic wrap and set aside. Heat 2 tablespoons of the oil in a wok or large skillet, until hot. Add the zucchini and stir-fry for 2 minutes. Add the bell pepper and garlic and cook for another 2 minutes. Add the asparagus and cook for 1 minute, then add the snow peas and cook for 2 minutes. Transfer the vegetables onto a plate.

Put the flour in a shallow dish and turn the fish slices in the flour until coated. Heat the remaining oil in the wok or skillet. Add the fish and stir-fry for 5 minutes, or until cooked to your taste (you may need to do this in batches). Transfer the fish to another plate.

Put the lemon sauce, lemongrass, and ginger in the wok or skillet. Add the fish and stir-fry over medium heat for a few seconds. Add the vegetables and stir-fry for 1 minute. Season, stir again, and remove from the heat. Transfer to warm plates and serve.

# thai fish burgers

| | | ingredients |
|---|---|---|
| | very easy | 12 oz/350 g haddock fillets, skinned and cut into small pieces    2 tbsp chopped fresh cilantro<br>1 tbsp peanut oil |
| | serves 4 | 2 tbsp chopped almonds<br>½ cup fresh bread crumbs    TO SERVE<br>½ onion, finely chopped    hamburger buns |
| | 15 minutes | 1 red chile, seeded and finely chopped    slices of tomato<br>1 egg white    selection of fresh salad greens<br>1 tbsp soy sauce |
| | 5–6 minutes | 1 tbsp finely chopped lemongrass |

Put the haddock, almonds, bread crumbs, onion, chile, egg white, soy sauce, lemongrass, and cilantro into a large bowl and stir together. Put the mixture into a food processor and process until thoroughly blended. Transfer to a clean counter and, using your hands, shape the mixture into flat, circular burger shapes.

Heat the oil in a skillet and add the burgers. Cook for about 5 minutes, turning once, until cooked through.

Remove from the heat. Serve with hamburger buns stuffed with tomato slices, crisp lettuce, and fresh salad greens.

# haddock nachos

| | |
|---|---|
| very easy | |
| serves 4 | |
| 10 minutes | |
| 15 minutes | |

**ingredients**

butter, for greasing
1 lb 7 oz/650 g haddock fillets, skinned
4 tomatoes, chopped
1 onion, chopped
1 tbsp lime juice
salt and pepper
1¾ oz/50 g tortilla chips

scant ½ cup cured semifirm cheese, grated

sprigs of fresh cilantro, to garnish

TO SERVE
½ cup sour cream
fresh crusty bread

Preheat the oven to 400°F/200°C. Grease a large baking dish with butter.

Rinse the haddock fillets under cold running water, then pat them dry with paper towels. Arrange the fillets in the bottom of the baking dish.

In a separate bowl, mix together the tomatoes, onion, and lime juice. Season with salt and pepper, then spread the mixture over the fish fillets. Scatter the tortilla chips over the top, then sprinkle over the grated cheese.

Bake in the center of the preheated oven for about 15 minutes. Remove from the oven and transfer to serving plates. Garnish with cilantro. Serve with the sour cream and fresh bread.

# mediterranean mussels in cream

| | |
|---|---|
| very easy | |
| serves 4 | |
| 15 minutes | |
| 20 minutes | |

### ingredients

2 tbsp butter
1 onion, chopped
2 scallions, chopped
2 garlic cloves, chopped
2 lb 4 oz/1 kg live mussels, soaked and
  cleaned (see page 20)
scant ½ cup dry white wine
3 tbsp chopped fresh parsley
²⁄₃ cup single cream

sprigs of fresh flatleaf parsley,
  to garnish

Melt the butter in a large pan over low heat. Add the onion, scallions, and garlic, and cook for 3 minutes until the onion has softened slightly. Increase the heat to medium, add the mussels, cover the pan, and cook for 4–5 minutes.

Remove the pan from the heat. Using a slotted spoon, lift out the mussels and discard any that have not opened. Set the remaining mussels to one side. Return the pan to the heat, stir in the wine and parsley, and bring to a boil. Continue to cook, stirring, for about 10 minutes.

Arrange the mussels in serving bowls, then remove the sauce from the heat. Stir in the cream, pour the sauce over the mussels, garnish with parsley sprigs, and serve.

# asian deep-fried shrimp

| | |
|---|---|
| very easy | |
| serves 4 | |
| 10 minutes | |
| 10–12 minutes | |

## ingredients

4 tbsp chili oil
4 scallions, trimmed and finely chopped
1 lb/450 g fresh shrimp, peeled and deveined
7 oz/200 g canned water chestnuts, drained and sliced
1 tbsp freshly grated lemongrass
1 red bell pepper, seeded and finely chopped

1 small red chile, seeded and chopped
1 tbsp grated fresh gingerroot
2 tbsp rice wine or sherry
2 tbsp chopped fresh cilantro
salt and pepper

GARNISH
fresh cilantro, finely chopped
slices of lime

freshly cooked jasmine rice, to serve

Heat the oil in a skillet and add the scallions. Cook over medium heat for 3 minutes until slightly softened.

Add the shrimp, water chestnuts, lemongrass, bell pepper, chile, ginger, rice wine or sherry, and cilantro. Season with salt and pepper. Cook, stirring, for 5–7 minutes, or according to your taste. Garnish with finely chopped cilantro and slices of lime, and serve with freshly cooked jasmine rice.

# spicy crab tortillas

| | | ingredients | |
|---|---|---|---|
| | very easy | 1 tbsp chili oil | 8 small wheat or corn tortillas |
| | | 1 large onion, coarsely chopped | |
| | serves 4 | 2 garlic cloves, chopped | sprigs of fresh cilantro, to garnish |
| | | 9 oz/250 g canned or freshly cooked | ½ cup sour cream, to serve |
| | | crab meat | |
| | | 1 small red chile, seeded and finely | |
| | 10 minutes | chopped | |
| | | 2 tomatoes, chopped | |
| | | 1 tbsp chopped fresh cilantro | |
| | 15 minutes | salt and pepper | |

Heat the oil in a skillet and add the onion and garlic. Cook over medium heat for 3–4 minutes, until the onion is slightly softened.

Add the crab meat, chile, tomatoes, and cilantro. Season with salt and pepper. Cook, stirring, for 10 minutes, or according to your taste. About a minute before the crab is ready, warm the tortillas in a dry skillet for a few seconds.

Remove the crab mixture and the tortillas from the heat. Spread a spoonful of sour cream into each tortilla, then add some of the crab mixture and roll up. Garnish with sprigs of fresh cilantro and serve at once.

# devilled shrimp

| | |
|---|---|
| very easy | |
| serves 4 | |
| 10 minutes | |
| 10–12 minutes | |

**ingredients**

4 tbsp peanut oil
4 scallions, trimmed and finely
  chopped
1 lb/450 g fresh shrimp, peeled and
  deveined
1 small red chile, seeded and finely
  chopped
2 tbsp sherry

pinch of paprika
1 tsp red food coloring, optional
salt and pepper

fresh cilantro stalks, finely sliced,
  to garnish

freshly boiled rice, to serve

Heat the oil in a skillet and add the scallions. Cook over medium heat for 3 minutes, until slightly softened.

Add the shrimp, chile, sherry, paprika, red food coloring (if using), and season with salt and pepper to taste. Cook, stirring, for about 5–7 minutes, or according to your taste. Garnish with finely sliced cilantro stalks and serve with freshly boiled rice.

# broiled sardines
# with lemon & cilantro

| | | ingredients | |
|---|---|---|---|
| very easy | | 12 sardines, scaled and gutted | 2 tbsp white wine vinegar |
| | | 1 tbsp olive oil | 4 tbsp chopped fresh cilantro |
| serves 4 | | | pepper |
| | | DRESSING | |
| | | 1 garlic clove, finely chopped | GARNISH |
| | | 3 scallions, trimmed and sliced | slices of fresh lemon |
| 10 minutes | | ½ cup extra-virgin olive oil | sprigs of fresh cilantro |
| | | 4 tbsp lemon juice | |
| 6 minutes | | | |

Preheat the broiler to medium. Rinse the fish inside and out under cold running water. Drain, then pat dry with paper towels.

To make the dressing, put the garlic, scallions, olive oil, lemon juice, vinegar, and cilantro into a small bowl and mix together well. Season with plenty of pepper and set aside.

Line a broiler pan with aluminum foil, then brush the foil with a little olive oil. Arrange the sardines on the foil, then spoon some of the dressing inside each fish. Brush more dressing on the top of the sardines and cook under the preheated broiler for about 3 minutes. Turn the fish over, brush with more dressing, and cook for another 3 minutes, or until cooked through.

Remove from the broiler, transfer to individual serving plates, and garnish with lemon slices and cilantro sprigs.

# crab & citrus salsa

| | |
|---|---|
| very easy | |
| serves 4 | |
| 10 minutes + 30 minutes to chill | |
| — | |

### ingredients

9 oz/250 g canned or freshly cooked
   crab meat
1 red bell pepper, seeded and chopped
4 tomatoes, chopped
3 scallions, trimmed and chopped
1 tbsp chopped fresh flatleaf parsley
1 red chile, seeded and chopped
3 tbsp lime juice
3 tbsp orange juice
salt and pepper

GARNISH
sprigs of fresh flatleaf parsley
wedges of lime

TO SERVE
carrots, cut into short, thin sticks
celery stalks, cut into short, thin sticks
tortilla chips

Put the crab meat, bell pepper, tomatoes, scallions, parsley, and chile into a large, nonmetallic (glass or ceramic) bowl, which will not react with acid. Add the lime juice and orange juice, season with salt and pepper, and mix well. Cover with plastic wrap and refrigerate for 30 minutes to allow the flavors to combine.

Remove the salsa from the refrigerator. Garnish with parsley sprigs and wedges of lime, and serve with carrots, celery, and tortilla chips for dipping.

# scallop bake

| | | ingredients | |
|---|---|---|---|
| <br>very easy | 3½ oz/100 g dried tagliatelle<br>2 tbsp butter, plus extra for greasing<br>1 lb 2 oz/500 g scallops<br>2 tbsp all-purpose flour<br>2 tbsp milk<br>1 cup single cream<br>salt and pepper | 3½ oz/100 g cooked ham, diced<br>2 scallions, trimmed and finely<br>  chopped<br>1 oz/ 25 g Parmesan cheese, freshly<br>  grated<br><br>TO SERVE<br>selection of salad greens<br>slices of fresh bread | |
| serves 4 | | | |
| 10 minutes | | | |
| 25 minutes | | | |

Cook the tagliatelle in a pan of salted boiling water for 10 minutes, or according to the instructions on the package. The pasta should be tender but still firm to the bite. While the pasta is cooking, preheat the oven to 350°F/180°C. Grease a large baking dish with butter. Bring a pan of water to a boil, then add the scallops and cook them for 2 minutes. Drain the scallops and set aside.

Put the remaining butter into a pan and melt it gently over low heat. Add the flour and cook, stirring, for 2 minutes. Pour in the milk, then stir in the cream. Season with salt and pepper and simmer for another 2 minutes.

Drain the tagliatelle and arrange on the bottom of the baking dish. Layer the scallops over the top, followed by the ham and scallions. Pour over the cream sauce, then sprinkle over the Parmesan cheese. Bake in the center of the preheated oven for about 15 minutes until golden. Serve with salad greens and slices of bread.

# sautéed shrimp with whiskey

| | |
|---|---|
| very easy | |
| serves 4 | |
| 10 minutes | |
| 8–10 minutes | |

**ingredients**

½ cup all-purpose flour
pinch of salt
pinch of paprika
1 lb 9 oz/700 g fresh shrimp, peeled
  and deveined
4 tbsp vegetable oil
3 garlic cloves, finely chopped
1 scallion, trimmed and finely chopped

2 tbsp chopped fresh cilantro
1 tbsp chopped fresh marjoram
4 tbsp whiskey
pepper

TO SERVE
crisp mixed salad
slices of French bread

Put the flour, salt, and paprika into a large bowl and mix together well. Add the shrimp and turn them in the mixture until coated.

Heat the oil in a skillet and add the shrimp, garlic, scallion, herbs, and whiskey. Season with pepper and stir together. Cook over medium heat, turning frequently, for 5 minutes. Remove the skillet from the heat and arrange the shrimp mixture on a heatproof serving dish.

To finish, place the dish under a broiler preheated to medium and cook for 2–3 minutes. Serve immediately with a crisp mixed salad and French bread.

# entrées

The dishes in this chapter are truly a feast
for the eyes and the palate. Inspiration for
these recipes has come from places as
diverse as the Scottish Highlands and the
Far East. From kedgeree to curry, and from
gratin to barbecue grill, the sheer variety of
ingredients and cooking methods in this
section will entice experienced cooks and
novices alike, and provide a culinary treat
that everyone will remember.

# broiled halibut with garlic butter

| | | **ingredients** |
|---|---|---|
| extremely easy | 4 halibut fillets, about 6 oz/175 g each<br>6 tbsp butter<br>2 garlic cloves, finely chopped<br>salt and pepper | GARNISH<br>sprigs of fresh parsley<br>thin strips of orange zest |
| serves 4 | | TO SERVE<br>crisp salad greens<br>cherry tomatoes, cut into slices |
| 5 minutes | | |
| 7–8 minutes | | |

Preheat the broiler to medium. Rinse the fish fillets under cold running water, then pat dry with paper towels.

Grease a shallow, heatproof dish with butter, then arrange the fish in it. Season with salt and pepper.

In a separate bowl, mix together the remaining butter with the garlic. Arrange pieces of the garlic butter all over the fish, then transfer to the broiler. Cook for 7–8 minutes, turning once, until the fish is cooked through.

Remove the dish from the broiler. Using a spatula, remove the fillets from the dish and arrange on individual serving plates. Pour over the remaining melted butter from the dish, and garnish with sprigs of fresh parsley and strips of lemon zest. Serve with crisp salad greens and cherry tomato slices.

# asian rainbow trout

| | | ingredients | |
|---|---|---|---|
| | extremely easy | 4 rainbow trout fillets, about 6 oz/175 g each | GARNISH sprigs of fresh cilantro fresh coconut, grated |
| | serves 4 | 4 tbsp chili oil salt and pepper 2 tbsp lemon juice | freshly boiled rice, to serve |
| | 10 minutes | 1 garlic clove, finely chopped 1 tbsp finely grated fresh gingerroot 1 tbsp freshly grated lemongrass | |
| | 5–6 minutes | 1 tbsp chopped fresh cilantro | |

Preheat the broiler to medium. Rinse the fish fillets under cold running water, then pat dry with paper towels.

Brush a shallow, heatproof dish with chili oil, then arrange the fish in it. Season the fish with salt and pepper.

In a separate bowl, mix together the remaining oil with the lemon juice, garlic, ginger, lemongrass, and cilantro. Spread the mixture all over the fish, then transfer the dish to the broiler. Cook for 5–6 minutes, turning once, or until the fish is cooked through.

Remove the dish from the broiler. Using a spatula, remove the fillets from the dish and arrange on individual serving plates. Pour over the remaining juices from the dish, garnish with cilantro sprigs and grated coconut, and serve with freshly boiled rice.

# grilled swordfish

| | | **ingredients** | |
|---|---|---|---|
| very easy | | 4 swordfish steaks, about 5½ oz/150 g each | GARNISH fresh cilantro, finely chopped |
| serves 4 | | salt and pepper | slices of lime |
| | | MARINADE | TO SERVE |
| 5 minutes + 1½ hours to marinate | | 3 tbsp rice wine or sherry | freshly baked potatoes in their skins |
| | | 3 tbsp chili oil | grilled corn cobs |
| | | 2 garlic cloves, finely chopped | fresh salad greens |
| | | juice of 1 lime | |
| 8 minutes | | 1 tbsp chopped fresh cilantro | |

To make the marinade, put the rice wine or sherry, oil, garlic, lime juice, and cilantro into a bowl and mix together well.

Rinse the fish fillets under cold running water, then pat dry with paper towels. Arrange the fish in a shallow, nonmetallic (glass or ceramic) dish, which will not react with acid. Season with salt and pepper, then pour over the marinade and turn the fish in the mixture until well coated. Cover with plastic wrap and refrigerate for about 1½ hours.

When the fish is thoroughly marinated, lift it out of the marinade and grill over hot coals for about 4 minutes. Turn the fish over, brush with more marinade, and grill on the other side for another 4 minutes, or until cooked through.

Remove from the barbecue grill and garnish with chopped fresh cilantro and slices of lime. Serve with baked potatoes in their skins, grilled corn cobs, and fresh salad greens.

# steamed sea bream with ginger

| | | ingredients | |
|---|---|---|---|
| easy | | 1 lb 2 oz/500 g sea bream fillets (if unavailable, use yellow perch, porgy, or red snapper instead) | 1 tbsp finely grated lemon zest<br>1 tbsp finely grated fresh gingerroot |
| serves 4 | | 1 garlic clove, finely chopped<br>1 small red chile, seeded and finely chopped | GARNISH<br>sprigs of fresh cilantro<br>wedges of lemon |
| 15 minutes | | 2 tbsp Thai fish sauce (nam pla)<br>3 tbsp lemon juice | TO SERVE |
| 10 minutes | | scant ½ cup fish bouillon<br>3 scallions, trimmed and finely sliced | freshly cooked egg noodles<br>fresh bread rolls, optional |

Rinse the fish fillets under cold running water, then pat dry with paper towels. Make several fairly deep diagonal cuts into the fish on both sides. Put the fish on a heatproof plate that is slightly smaller than your wok. The plate should have a rim.

In a separate bowl, mix together the garlic, chile, fish sauce, lemon juice, and bouillon. Pour this mixture over the fish. Scatter over the scallions, lemon zest, and ginger.

Fill a large wok with boiling water up to a depth of 1½ inches/ 4 cm. Bring it back to a boil, then set a rack or trivet inside the wok. Put the plate of fish on top of the rack, then cover the wok with a lid. Lower the heat a little and steam the fish for about 10 minutes or until cooked through.

Lift out the fish and arrange on a platter of freshly cooked egg noodles. Garnish with cilantro sprigs and lemon wedges. Serve with fresh bread rolls (if using).

# salmon with brandy sauce

| | |
|---|---|
| very easy | |
| serves 4 | |
| 10 minutes | |
| 25 minutes | |

### ingredients

1 lb 7 oz/650 g salmon steaks
3 tbsp butter
1 garlic clove, finely chopped
1 onion, chopped
1 leek, trimmed and finely sliced
2 tbsp chopped fresh cilantro
4 tbsp brandy
6 tbsp light cream
1 tbsp lime juice
salt and pepper

GARNISH
fresh cilantro, chopped
Parmesan cheese, freshly grated
8 cherry tomatoes, halved and broiled

TO SERVE
freshly cooked tagliatelle
slices of fresh bread

Rinse the fish steaks under cold running water, then pat dry with paper towels.

Melt 2 tablespoons of the butter in a large skillet over medium heat. Add the fish and cook for 3 minutes, then turn over and cook on the other side for another 3 minutes. Using a spatula, lift out the fish and keep it warm.

Melt the remaining butter in the skillet over medium heat, then add the garlic, onion, and leek. Cook for 4 minutes until slightly softened, then stir in the cilantro, brandy, cream, and lime juice. Season with salt and pepper. Continue to cook, stirring, for 10–12 minutes.

Divide the tagliatelle between serving plates. Arrange the fish on top. Pour over the sauce. Garnish with chopped fresh cilantro, grated Parmesan, and the broiled tomatoes. Serve with slices of fresh bread.

# mixed fish curry

| | | ingredients | |
|---|---|---|---|
| | very easy | 3 tbsp butter | 1 tbsp orange juice |
| | | 3 garlic cloves, chopped | 1 tbsp chopped fresh cilantro |
| | serves 4 | 2 shallots, chopped | 1 tbsp chopped fresh parsley |
| | | 1 small red chile, seeded and chopped | salt and pepper |
| | | 4 tbsp grated coconut | GARNISH |
| | 10 minutes | pinch of cayenne pepper | fresh cilantro, chopped |
| | | 1 tsp mild curry powder | slices of orange |
| | | ½ tsp garam masala | |
| | | 1½ cups water | TO SERVE |
| | 25 minutes | 12 oz/350 g cod fillets | freshly boiled rice |
| | | 12 oz/350 g haddock fillets | pappadams (sold in Asian/Indian stores) |

Melt the butter in a large skillet over low heat. Add the garlic and shallots and cook, stirring, for about 3 minutes until slightly softened. Add the chile, grated coconut, cayenne pepper, curry powder, and garam masala, and cook for another 2 minutes. Stir in the water and bring to a boil, then lower the heat and simmer for 7–8 minutes.

Rinse the fish under cold running water, then pat dry with paper towels. Add the fish to the pan with the orange juice and herbs, and season with salt and pepper. Simmer for another 7–8 minutes, until the fish is cooked through.

Arrange the freshly boiled rice on serving plates, then spoon over the curry, dividing the fish fillets evenly between the plates. Garnish with chopped fresh cilantro and slices of orange. Serve at once with crisp plain pappadams.

# fish kedgeree

| | | ingredients | |
|---|---|---|---|
| very easy | | 3 tbsp butter | 1 ¼ cups milk |
| | | 2 shallots, chopped | ½ tsp garam masala |
| serves 4 | | 1 leek, trimmed and finely sliced | salt and pepper |
| | | 1 ½ cups brown rice | Napa cabbage, finely shredded, |
| | | 2 ½ cups fish bouillon | to garnish |
| 10 minutes | | 7 oz/200 g salmon fillets | |
| | | 7 oz/200 g cured haddock fillets | fresh bread rolls, to serve |
| 30 minutes | | | |

Preheat the oven to 375°F/190°C. Melt the butter in a large skillet over low heat. Add the shallots and leek and cook, stirring, for about 4 minutes, until slightly softened. Add the rice, then stir in the bouillon and bring to a boil.

Transfer the shallot mixture to a large, ovenproof casserole dish. Cover and bake in the center of the preheated oven for about 25 minutes, until all the liquid has been absorbed.

About 5 minutes before the end of the cooking time, rinse the fish fillets under cold running water, then pat dry with paper towels. Pour the milk into a pan and bring to a boil. Add the fish and poach for 5–6 minutes, until tender.

Remove the rice from the oven. Drain the fish, discard the milk, and flake into small pieces using a fork. Add the fish and garam masala to the rice, and season with salt and pepper. Stir together well and garnish with shredded Napa cabbage. Serve with bread rolls.

# mixed fish & potato pie

| | | ingredients | |
|---|---|---|---|
| easy | | 12 oz/350 g haddock fillets | 1 tbsp chopped fresh cilantro |
| | | 12 oz/350 g halibut fillets | 2 onions, 1 grated and 1 sliced |
| | | 12 oz/350 g salmon fillets | salt and pepper |
| serves 4 | | 2½ cups milk | ¾ cup grated colby cheese |
| | | ½ cup brandy | |
| | | 2 lb 4 oz/1 kg potatoes, sliced | selection of freshly cooked vegetables, |
| 15 minutes | | 5 tbsp butter, plus extra for greasing | to serve |
| | | 3 tbsp all-purpose flour | |
| | | 1 tbsp chopped fresh parsley | |
| 1 hour 10 minutes | | | |

Preheat the oven to 400°F/200°C. Rinse all the fish, then pat dry with paper towels. Pour the milk into a pan and bring to a boil. Add the haddock and halibut and cook gently for 10 minutes. Lift out and set aside. Reserve the milk. In a separate pan, cook the salmon in the brandy over low heat for 10 minutes. Lift out and set aside. Reserve the cooking liquid. Cut all the fish into small chunks.

Cook the potatoes in a pan of lightly salted water for 15 minutes. Meanwhile, in another pan, melt the butter over low heat, stir in the flour, and cook for 1 minute. Stir in the reserved milk and brandy liquid to make a smooth sauce. Bring to a boil, then simmer for 10 minutes. Remove from the heat and stir in the herbs. Drain and mash the potatoes, then add the grated onion. Season. Grease a large pie dish with butter, then add the fish. Top with sliced onion. Pour over enough sauce to cover. Top with mashed potato, then grated cheese. Bake for 30 minutes. Serve with cooked vegetables.

# cod puff pie

| | | **ingredients** | |
|---|---|---|---|
| easy | | 1 lb 9 oz/700 g cod fillets | 2 tbsp chopped fresh basil |
| | | 2½ cups fish bouillon | 1 tbsp sherry |
| serves 4 | | 9 oz/250 g potatoes, sliced | all-purpose flour, for dusting |
| | | 2 tbsp butter | 1 package frozen puff pastry dough, |
| | | 1 onion, sliced | thawed |
| | | 1 garlic clove, chopped | salt and pepper |
| 20 minutes | | 1 carrot, sliced | 1 tbsp milk |
| | | 2 celery stalks, trimmed and sliced | |
| | | 3½ oz/100 g crimini mushrooms, wiped | TO SERVE |
| | | and sliced | crisp salad greens |
| 1 hour | | 4 tomatoes, sliced | freshly cooked snow peas |

Rinse the cod and pat dry. Bring the bouillon to a boil, add the cod, and simmer for 10 minutes. Drain and cut into chunks. Meanwhile, cook the potatoes in salted water for 5 minutes. Drain. Melt half the butter in a skillet over low heat. Add the onion and garlic and cook for 3 minutes. Add the carrot and celery and cook for 5 minutes. Lift out the vegetables and set aside. Preheat the oven to 400°F/200°C.

Melt the remaining butter in the skillet. Add the mushrooms and tomatoes and cook for 7 minutes. Stir in the basil and sherry. Cook for 1 minute. On a floured counter, roll out enough dough to line a large pie dish, with an overhang of 1 inch/2.5 cm. Put some tomato mixture into the dish. Top with a layer of cod, then a vegetable layer, then a potato layer. Repeat the layers to fill the pie. Season. Top with dough, trim and crimp, and make a slit in the top. Decorate with dough fish shapes and brush with milk. Bake for 30 minutes. Serve with crisp salad green and freshly cooked snow peas.

# haddock cobbler

| | | **ingredients** | |
|---|---|---|---|
| easy | | 12 oz/350 g cod fillets | PIE DOUGH |
| | | 12 oz/350 g haddock fillets | 4 tbsp butter |
| serves 4 | | scant 2 cups milk | 1 cup all-purpose flour |
| | | 1 bay leaf | 1 tsp baking powder |
| | | 4 tbsp butter | pinch of nutmeg |
| 25 minutes | | 6 tbsp all-purpose flour | 1 egg yolk |
| | | 1 tbsp chopped fresh dill | 4 tbsp milk |
| | | 1 tbsp chopped fresh parsley | TO SERVE |
| 50 minutes | | 7 oz/ 200 g grated colby cheese | cherry tomatoes, halved |
| | | salt and pepper | freshly cooked green beans |

Rinse the fish and pat dry. Pour the milk into a large pan, add the bay leaf, and bring to a boil. Lower the heat, add the fish, and cook gently for 10 minutes. Lift out the fish and set aside. Discard the bay leaf. Reserve the milk. Melt the butter in a pan. Stir in the flour and cook gently for 1 minute. Gradually stir in enough reserved milk to make a smooth sauce. Bring to a boil, then simmer for 5 minutes. Remove from the heat, stir in the herbs and half the cheese, and season. Preheat the oven to 400°F/200°C. Cut the fish into chunks.

In a separate bowl, rub the butter into the flour, then add the baking powder and nutmeg. Stir in the egg yolk and enough milk to make a pliable dough. Roll out to $1/2$ inch/1 cm thick. Using a cookie cutter, cut out circles about 2–3 inches/5–7.5 cm in diameter. Put the fish chunks into a pie dish. Pour over the sauce and top with the dough circles. Sprinkle over the remaining cheese. Bake for 30 minutes. Serve with halved cherry tomatoes and freshly cooked green beans.

# baked dover sole
# with vegetables

| | | | **ingredients** | |
|---|---|---|---|---|
| | very easy | 4 Dover sole fillets, about | | 2 tbsp chopped fresh basil |
| | | 1 lb 7 oz/650 g each | | salt and pepper |
| | serves 4 | 3 tbsp extra-virgin olive oil | | 6 tbsp freshly grated Parmesan |
| | | 3 shallots, chopped | | |
| | | 1 garlic clove, chopped | | black and green olives, pitted, |
| | | 1 zucchini, sliced | | to garnish |
| | 10 minutes | 2 scallions, trimmed and chopped | | |
| | | 15 oz/425 g canned plum tomatoes | | selection of freshly cooked vegetables, |
| | | 6 black olives, pitted and sliced | | to serve |
| | 50 minutes | 6 green olives, pitted and sliced | | |

Preheat the oven to 375°F/190°C. Rinse the fish fillets under cold running water and pat dry with paper towels.

Heat 2 tablespoons of the oil in a large skillet over low heat. Add the shallots and garlic, and cook, stirring, for about 3 minutes, until slightly softened. Add the zucchini and scallions, and cook for another 4 minutes, stirring. Add the tomatoes and their juice, and the olives and basil. Season with salt and pepper and simmer for another 10 minutes.

Brush a shallow, ovenproof baking dish with the remaining oil, then arrange the fish fillets in it. Remove the pan from the heat and pour the sauce over the fish. Sprinkle over the Parmesan and bake in the center of the preheated oven for about 30 minutes, or until the fish is cooked through.

Remove from the oven and transfer to serving plates. Garnish with black and green olives and serve with freshly cooked vegetables.

# mediterranean-style sea bass

| | | ingredients | |
|---|---|---|---|
| extremely easy | | 4 tbsp basil-flavored oil or extra-virgin olive oil<br>1 lb 10 oz/750 g sea bass fillets<br>12 black olives, pitted and cut into fourths<br>1 tbsp lemon juice<br>2 tbsp dry white wine | 2 tbsp chopped fresh basil<br>salt and pepper<br><br>GARNISH<br>wedges of lemon<br>sprigs of fresh basil<br><br>fresh mixed salad, to serve |
| serves 4 | | | |
| 5 minutes | | | |
| 8–10 minutes | | | |

Heat the oil in a large skillet over medium heat. Add the fish and cook for 5 minutes, turning once, or until cooked through.

Add the olives, lemon juice, wine, and basil to the pan, and season with salt and pepper. Cook for another 2 minutes, stirring.

Arrange the mixed salad on serving plates. Remove the pan from the heat and use a spatula to lift out the fish and place it on top of the lettuce. Pour over any remaining juices from the pan, garnish with lemon wedges and sprigs of fresh basil, and serve at once.

# roasted salmon
# with lemon & herbs

| | | |
|---|---|---|
| very easy | **ingredients** | |
| | 6 tbsp extra-virgin olive oil | GARNISH |
| serves 4 | 1 onion, sliced | slices of lemon |
| | 1 leek, trimmed and sliced | sprigs of fresh dill |
| | juice of ½ lemon | |
| | 2 tbsp chopped fresh parsley | freshly cooked baby spinach leaves, |
| 10 minutes | 2 tbsp chopped fresh dill | to serve |
| | salt and pepper | |
| | 1 lb 2 oz/500 g salmon fillets | |
| 15 minutes | | |

Preheat the oven to 400°F/200°C. Heat 1 tablespoon of the oil in a skillet over medium heat. Add the onion and leek and cook, stirring, for about 4 minutes, until slightly softened.

Meanwhile, put the remaining oil in a small bowl with the lemon juice and herbs, and season. Stir together well. Rinse the fish under cold running water, then pat dry with paper towels. Arrange the fish in a shallow, ovenproof baking dish.

Remove the skillet from the heat and spread the onion and leek over the fish. Pour the oil mixture over the top, ensuring that everything is well coated. Roast in the center of the preheated oven for about 10 minutes or until the fish is cooked through.

Arrange the cooked spinach on serving plates. Remove the fish and vegetables from the oven and arrange on top of the freshly cooked spinach. Garnish with lemon slices and sprigs of dill. Serve at once.

# roasted mackerel
# mediterranean-style

| | |
|---|---|
| very easy | |
| serves 4 | |
| 15 minutes | |
| 25 minutes | |

### ingredients

4 tbsp basil oil or extra-virgin olive oil
2 garlic cloves, chopped
1 onion, sliced
2 zucchini, trimmed and sliced
6 plum tomatoes, sliced
12 black olives, pitted and halved
1 tbsp tomato paste
4 tbsp red wine
scant ½ cup fish bouillon
2 tbsp chopped fresh parsley

2 tbsp chopped fresh basil
salt and pepper
4 large mackerel, cleaned

GARNISH
slices of lemon
sprigs of fresh basil

TO SERVE
freshly cooked spaghetti
fresh salad greens and scallions

Preheat the oven to 400°F/200°C. Heat 1 tablespoon of oil in a large skillet over medium heat. Add the garlic, onion, and zucchini and cook, stirring, for about 4 minutes.

Add the tomatoes, olives, tomato paste, wine, bouillon, and herbs. Season with salt and pepper and bring to a boil. Lower the heat to medium and cook, stirring, for 10 minutes.

Rinse the fish under cold running water, then pat dry with paper towels. Arrange the fish in a shallow, ovenproof baking dish. Remove the skillet from the heat and spread the tomato sauce over the fish. Roast in the center of the preheated oven for about 10 minutes or until the fish is cooked through.

Remove from the oven, arrange the fish in its sauce on plates of freshly cooked spaghetti, and garnish with lemon slices and sprigs of basil. Serve accompanied by fresh salad greens and scallions.

# shrimp & haddock curry

| | | **ingredients** | |
|---|---|---|---|
| very easy | | 2 tbsp vegetable oil | ½ cup fish bouillon |
| | | 2 garlic cloves, chopped | salt and pepper |
| | | 4 shallots, chopped | 1 lb/450 g haddock fillets, skinned |
| serves 4 | | 1 tbsp grated fresh gingerroot | 12 oz/350 g shrimp, peeled and |
| | | 1 tsp mild curry powder | deveined |
| | | 1 red bell pepper, seeded and chopped | 5 tbsp plain yogurt |
| 15 minutes | | 7 oz/200 g canned red kidney beans, drained | fresh coconut, grated, to garnish |
| | | 3 tomatoes, chopped | TO SERVE |
| 25 minutes | | 3 tbsp grated fresh coconut | freshly boiled rice |
| | | 3 tbsp chopped fresh cilantro | fresh nan bread |

Heat the oil in a large pan over low heat. Add the garlic, shallots, ginger, and curry powder, and cook, stirring, for about 4 minutes, until the shallots have softened slightly.

Add the red bell pepper, kidney beans, tomatoes, coconut, and cilantro. Stir in the bouillon. Season with salt and pepper and bring to a boil. Lower the heat and simmer, stirring occasionally, for 15 minutes.

Rinse the fish fillets under cold running water, then pat dry with paper towels. Cut the fish into small chunks, then add it to the pan. Cook for 2 minutes. Add the shrimp and cook for another 3 minutes, or until all the fish is cooked through, but do not overcook.

Remove from the heat and stir in the yogurt. Arrange the fish curry on plates of freshly boiled rice. Garnish with grated coconut and serve with nan bread.

# seafood gratin

| | |
|---|---|
| easy | |
| serves 4 | |
| 15 minutes | |
| 1 hour | |

**ingredients**

1 lb/450 g cod fillets
8 oz/225 g shrimp, peeled and
  deveined
8 oz/225 g scallops
3 tbsp extra-virgin olive oil
1 garlic clove, chopped
4 scallions, trimmed and chopped
1 zucchini, sliced
15 oz/425 g canned plum tomatoes

2 tbsp chopped fresh basil
1 cup fresh bread crumbs
scant ½ cup grated colby cheese
salt and pepper

selection of freshly cooked broccoli and
  cauliflower, to serve

Bring a large pan of water to a boil, then lower the heat to medium. Rinse the cod, pat dry with paper towels, and add to the pan. Cook for 5 minutes. Add the shrimp and cook for 3 minutes, then add the scallops and cook for 2 minutes. Drain, refresh under cold running water, and drain again. Preheat the oven to 375°F/190°C.

Heat 2 tablespoons of the oil in a skillet over low heat. Add the garlic and scallions and cook, stirring, for 3 minutes. Add the zucchini and cook for 3 minutes, then add the tomatoes and their juice, and the basil. Season and simmer for 10 minutes.

Brush a shallow baking dish with the remaining oil and arrange the seafood in it. Remove the pan from the heat and pour the sauce over the fish. Scatter over the bread crumbs and top with cheese. Bake for 30 minutes, until golden.

Remove from the oven and serve with broccoli and cauliflower.